THE HOUSE DIARY

For All Home Owners

THE HOUSE DIARY

For All Home Owners

Enjoy your book.

Lottie Brelsford

March 19, 1992

WOW • WADDA, CO.®, PUBLICATIONS
PORTLAND, OREGON
U.S.A.

All inquires should be addressed to:

Wow • Wadda, Co.
P.O. Box 12223
Portland, OR 97212-0223
503 249-0051

International Standard Book No. 0-9631632-8-0

**Brelsford, Lottie Knudson
The house diary, for all home owners**

**Printed in the United States of America
This book is printed on recycled paper.**

THIS BOOK IS DEDICATED TO

FRIENDS AND NEIGHBORS ON OAKCREST WAY

WHO LOVE THEIR HOMES AND ARE PROUD
TO BE PART OF OUR NEIGHBORHOOD

Acknowledgments

This book would not have become a reality without the encouragement, support and professional suggestions of many. Special thanks to Carter and JoAnn George, and Glen and Evelyn Haley.

Thanks also to the many friends, neighbors, and family members who added their best wishes that **The House Diary** would become a successful venture. Special thanks to my daughter, Mary, for all her help, and to Rick Shannon for his creative expertise.

About the Author

LOTTIE KNUDSON BRELSFORD, from a small town in Northern Minnesota, obtained her B.S. in Home Economics from the University of Minnesota in 1935. She later worked as a Home Supervisor for Farm Security Administration (now called Farm and Home) and as a County 4-H leader. During World War II she was a supervisor for the Office of Price Administration. It was also during the war that she met and married her husband, John, who served in the RAF. After John finished college in Chicago they settled in the Pacific Northwest. It was during the 5 1/2-year period when John was on kidney dialysis, and after his death in 1985, that Lottie says she truly came to appreciate her home, wonderful neighbors, and friends.

Credits

Wes Cropper – Cover Design
B & B Litho – Printing
Lincoln & Allen – Bindery
Northwest Association of Book Publishers
Mocha Publishing
Janice Arnold – Editing and Page Design

THE HOUSE DIARY

Contents

—————— 1 ▐░▌ 1 ——————

BASIC INFORMATION ABOUT THE HOUSE AND PROPERTY

—————— 2 ▐░▌ 2 ——————

NEIGHBORHOOD AND COMMUNITY

──────── **3** 🏛 **3** ────────

FINANCIAL OVERVIEW

──────── **4** 🏛 **4** ────────

THE HOUSE RESUME

──────── **5** 🏛 **5** ────────

THE HOUSE DIARY

Preface

When I was informed my house needed a new roof I was shocked. It seemed that it had been replaced only yesterday. Before his death, my husband, John, had taken care of house maintenance. My subsequent search for information on the old roofing job made me realize how much I needed a simple, handy system to record house improvements.

The search for an existing system led to the creation of **The House Diary**. Books I found for keeping records were either too much work or too complicated to be of value to me, or they were not organized to be easy to use. I am too busy to make household record-keeping a full-time job. I enjoy quilting and other hobbies and have responsibilities beyond running my house. I realized that others must have needs similar to mine, so here is my solution – **The House Diary.**

The House Diary has been prepared for houses of all sizes, styles, and values, and for owners of any income range.

Not only is this diary a simple way to keep track of projects and costs, it will be especially valuable if you decide to sell your home. All the improvements you have made to your house and the costs for upkeep and running the house will be in one place. You might want to leave the book with the new owners of your house. (Of course, you can only hope that the owners of *your* new home have left a copy of **The House Diary**.)

Although this information does not relate to the house's physical properties, you might want to include special events that happen in your house such as births, weddings, and reunions. I record the first snowfall on the mountains, spotting quail and babies in the back yard, first sunbath on the patio, when it's time to wrap the pipes, the hottest day on record for the year. Use your imagination.

Lottie Knudson Brelsford
December 12, 1991

"The strength of a nation is derived from the integrity of its homes."
– Confucius (*c.* 551-479 B.C.)

Basic Information

This House Belongs to

_____

Address

_____

Here's the House!

Attach photographs or make a drawing of your house.

History and Photographs of the House

Place and identify old photographs of the house and property.

History and Photographs of the House

More old photographs of the house and property.

History and Photographs of the House

Historical information about the house.

The House and Other Structures

Basic facts about the house that are interesting and important to keep track of for future reference.

The House

Original Owner _____

Architect _____

Builder/Subcontractors _____

_____

_____

Style of Architecture *(e.g. ranch, Tudor)* _____

Dimensions _____

Roof Material *(e.g. cedar shake, tile)* _____

Basic Construction *(e.g. wood frame, concrete)* _____

Siding *(e.g. aluminum, stucco, wood)* _____

_____

Year Completed _____

Original Cost _____

Location of Important Documents _____

_____

_____

_____

The House and Other Structures

Other Structures on the Land

_____

_____

_____

_____

_____

_____

_____

_____

_____

_____

_____

_____

_____

_____

_____

_____

_____

Special Features of the House

Keep information useful in selling the house here. Those features of your house that you find special — for example, garage close to kitchen makes unloading groceries easy; large closets and plenty of storage space; great view — may be special to others as well.

House and Room Plans

Use these graph pages for drawing the rooms in your house to scale. Accurate diagrams help in estimating paint, carpeting, and wall covering amounts. Furniture and decorating plans can be penciled in.

Scale: ☐ = ____ *ft.*

House and Room Plans

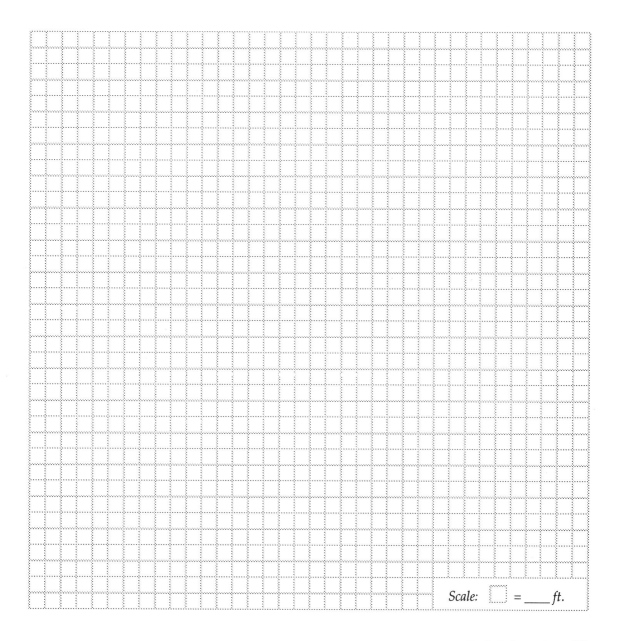

Scale: ☐ = ____ *ft.*

House and Room Plans

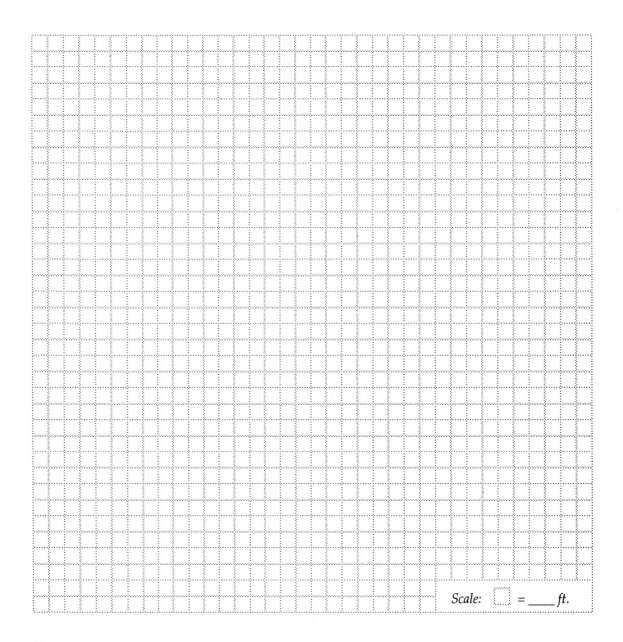

Scale: ☐ = ____ *ft.*

House and Room Plans

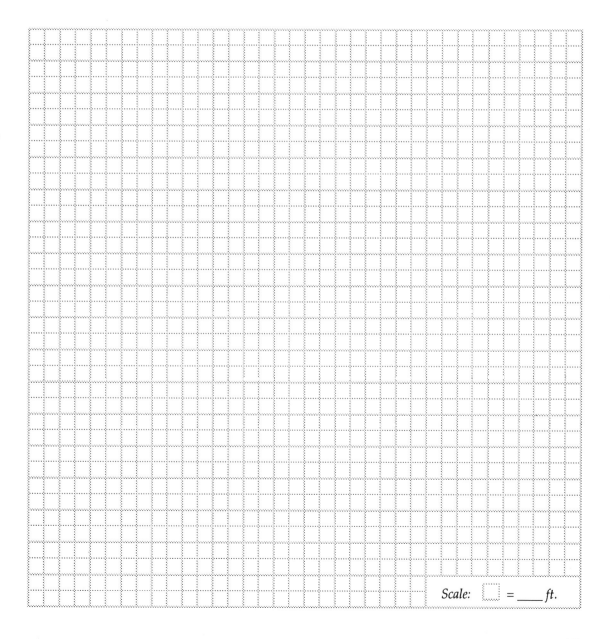

Scale: ☐ = ____ *ft.*

House and Room Plans

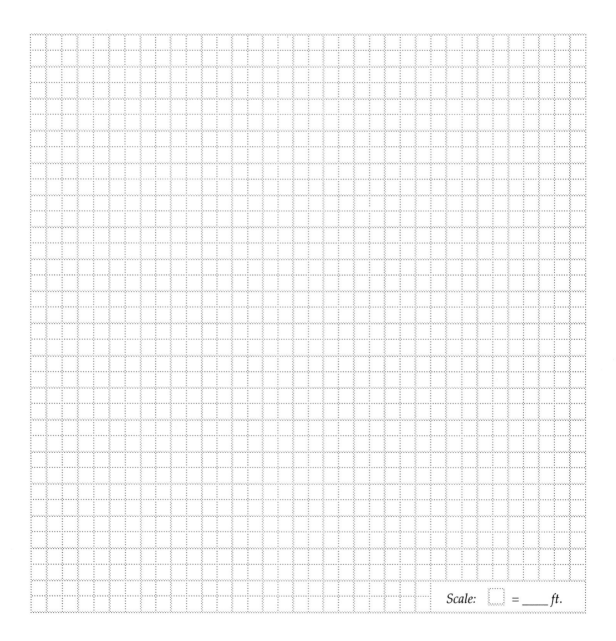

Scale: ☐ = _____ *ft.*

House and Room Plans

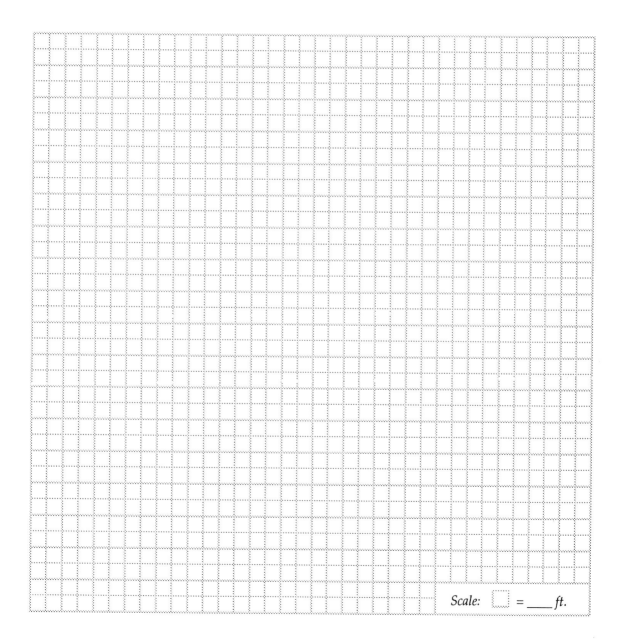

Scale: ☐ = _____ ft.

Fuse or Circuit Breaker Diagram

Draw and label your fuse or circuit breaker box in this space. This will save time turning switches off and on when you blow a fuse. It will also be insurance against faded, unreadable labels attached to the box.

Location of Box:_____

Switch # _____   ON OFF   ON OFF   Switch # _____

_____   □ □   □ □   _____

_____   _____

Switch # _____   ON OFF   ON OFF   Switch # _____

_____   □ □   □ □   _____

_____   _____

Switch # _____   ON OFF   ON OFF   Switch # _____

_____   □ □   □ □   _____

_____   _____

Switch # _____   ON OFF   ON OFF   Switch # _____

_____   □ □   □ □   _____

_____   _____

Switch # _____   ON OFF   ON OFF   Switch # _____

_____   □ □   □ □   _____

_____   _____

Switch # _____   ON OFF   ON OFF   Switch # _____

_____   □ □   □ □   _____

_____   _____

Fuse or Circuit Breaker Diagram

Location of Box:_____

Switch # _____   ON OFF   ON OFF   **Switch #** _____
_____   ☐ ☐   ☐ ☐   _____
_____   _____

Switch # _____   ON OFF   ON OFF   **Switch #** _____
_____   ☐ ☐   ☐ ☐   _____
_____   _____

Switch # _____   ON OFF   ON OFF   **Switch #** _____
_____   ☐ ☐   ☐ ☐   _____
_____   _____

Switch # _____   ON OFF   ON OFF   **Switch #** _____
_____   ☐ ☐   ☐ ☐   _____
_____   _____

Switch # _____   ON OFF   ON OFF   **Switch #** _____
_____   ☐ ☐   ☐ ☐   _____
_____   _____

Switch # _____   ON OFF   ON OFF   **Switch #** _____
_____   ☐ ☐   ☐ ☐   _____
_____   _____

The Property

Legal Description of the Property

_____

_____

_____

_____

_____

_____

Written Description of the Property
Include the lay-of-the-land; north, south, east, west orientation; elevation; and other pertinent information.

_____

_____

_____

_____

_____

_____

_____

_____

_____

The Property

County Property Appraisal

Tax Account Number _____

Taxes   Date: _____

              Land: _____

              House: _____   Total: _____

              Date: _____

              Land: _____

              House: _____   Total: _____

              Date: _____

              Land: _____

              House: _____   Total: _____

              Date: _____

              Land: _____

              House: _____   Total: _____

              Date: _____

              Land: _____

              House: _____   Total: _____

The Property

Survey Information

Land Lot Number _____

District _____

County _____

Plat Book Number _____

Date _____

Main Roads _____

Location of Information

Identify the city, county, or state offices where information on your property is recorded.

Name _____

Address _____

Phone Number _____

Name _____

Address _____

Phone Number _____

Name _____

Address _____

Phone Number _____

The Grounds

Location of Underground Services

Draw the diagram of where sewer, cable, and other underground systems lie. Include information on the location of the main shut offs.

The Grounds

General Plantings

The Grounds

Landscape Plans

Draw and label garden layout and use the space to plan future plantings.

The Grounds

Notes on Special Landscaping

_____

_____

_____

_____

_____

_____

_____

_____

_____

_____

_____

_____

_____

_____

_____

_____

_____

_____

_____

The Grounds

Special Landscape Plans

The Grounds

Other Outside Features

Include sidewalks, fences, swimming pool, deck, porches, and outdoor lighting.

Photographs of the House,
Other Structures and the Land

More Photos

More Photos

"The impersonal hand of government can never replace the helping hand of a neighbor."
– Hubert Humphrey (1911-1978)

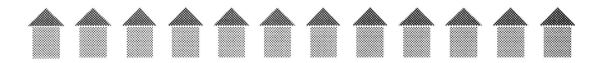

Neighborhood & Community

Locations of Services

Schools   **Telephone Numbers**

Pre-Schools _____   _____

_____   _____

Kindergarten _____   _____

_____   _____

Grade School _____   _____

_____   _____

Middle School/Junior High _____   _____

_____   _____

High School _____   _____

_____   _____

Technical/Vocational Schools _____   _____

_____   _____

Private Schools _____   _____

_____   _____

_____   _____

_____   _____

_____   _____

Locations of Services

Schools   **Telephone Numbers**

Community Colleges _____   _____

_____   _____

_____   _____

Universities _____   _____

_____   _____

_____   _____

Summer Schools _____   _____

_____   _____

_____   _____

Private Teachers _____   _____

_____   _____

_____   _____

_____   _____

_____   _____

_____   _____

_____   _____

Locations of Services

Buses / Bus Routes / Mass Transit _____

_____

_____

_____

_____

_____

_____

_____

Library _____

_____

_____

_____

Shopping _____

_____

_____

_____

_____

_____

Locations of Services

Banks _____

_____

_____

_____

Neighborhood Watch _____

_____

Police Station _____

_____

_____

Hospitals _____

_____

_____

Immediate Care Facilities _____

_____

_____

Churches _____

_____

_____

_____

Locations of Services

Recreation Facilities   **Telephone Numbers**

Swimming Pools _____   _____

_____   _____

Tennis Courts _____   _____

_____   _____

Parks and Playgrounds _____   _____

_____   _____

_____   _____

Picnic Facilities _____   _____

_____   _____

Bowling Alleys _____   _____

_____   _____

Ice Skating Rinks _____   _____

_____   _____

Roller Skating Rinks _____   _____

_____   _____

Skiing _____   _____

_____   _____

_____   _____

Locations of Services

Recreation Facilities   **Telephone Numbers**

Racquetball _____   _____

_____   _____

_____   _____

Basketball _____   _____

_____   _____

_____   _____

Baseball _____   _____

_____   _____

_____   _____

Soccer _____   _____

_____   _____

Health Clubs _____   _____

_____   _____

_____   _____

Other _____   _____

_____   _____

_____   _____

_____   _____

Locations of Services

Arts and Entertainment   **Telephone Numbers**

Movie Theaters _____   _____

_____   _____

_____   _____

_____   _____

_____   _____

_____   _____

Video Rentals _____   _____

_____   _____

_____   _____

Theaters _____   _____

_____   _____

_____   _____

Concert Halls _____   _____

_____   _____

_____   _____

Museums _____   _____

_____   _____

_____   _____

Locations of Services

Telephone Numbers

Ticket Outlets _____ _____

_____ _____

_____ _____

Restaurants _____ _____

_____ _____

_____ _____

_____ _____

_____ _____

Other _____ _____

_____ _____

_____ _____

_____ _____

_____ _____

_____ _____

_____ _____

_____ _____

Special Telephone Numbers

Utilities

Electric Company _____

Gas Company _____

Telephone Company _____

_____

Water Company _____

Other _____

_____

State, County, and Municipal Services

Animal Control _____

City Hall _____

Highway Patrol _____

Sanitation Department _____

Sheriff _____

Snow Removal _____

Streets/Highways _____

Other _____

Polling/Voting Precinct _____

_____

Special Telephone Numbers

Home/Property Care and Maintenance

Appliance Repair _____

_____

Cable Television _____

Carpenter _____

Carpet Installer _____

Carpet/Upholstery Cleaner _____

Chimney Sweep _____

Drapery Maker _____

Decorator _____

Electrician _____

Exterminator/Pest Control _____

Firewood Delivery _____

Gardener _____

Gutter Cleaner _____

Hardware Store _____

Housekeeper _____

Lawn Maintenance _____

Locksmith _____

Special Telephone Numbers

Newspaper Delivery _____

Painter, Interior _____

Painter, Exterior _____

Paper Hanger _____

Pool Maintenance _____

Plumber _____

Recyclers _____

Roofer _____

Septic Service _____

Tree Surgeon _____

Upholsterer _____

Window Washer _____

Other _____

_____

_____

_____

_____

_____

Special Telephone Numbers

Other Services

Bakery _____

Caterer _____

Delicatessen _____

Florist _____

Hairdresser _____

Insurance Agent _____

Kennel _____

Real Estate Agent _____

Taxi _____

Time-of-Day _____

Travel Conditions _____

Veterinarian _____

Weather _____

Take-out Food _____

_____

_____

_____

_____

Special Telephone Numbers

Neighbors

Names	Address	Telephone Number

Special Telephone Numbers

Neighbors

Names	Address	Telephone Number

Other Neighborhood References

Who has what in the neighborhood?

One of the best aspects of living in a good neighborhood with great neighbors is the opportunity to share. List whatever gets shared in your neighborhood, the extra card tables and chairs, the punch bowl and glasses, the playpen, the shrub clippers, or other tools. Be sure to include the owner's name – it makes it easy to return borrowed items punctually and without an embarrassing delay.

Other Neighborhood References

What's on loan?

List the items you've loaned to neighbors, when you expect it returned, or favors that you owe the neighbors.

Instructions for House-Sitters

Your house-sitter is only as well-prepared as the instructions you leave behind. Think ahead to what someone looking after your house needs to know – what if a water pipe breaks, or gas leaks? Are you expecting any deliveries that the sitter needs to take care of? Do you have any quirky appliances in your home that need special instructions?

Water Shut-Off Valve _____

Hot Water Shut-Off _____

Gas Shut-Off _____

Heat/Thermostat _____

Services/Deliveries Expected _____

_____

_____

_____

Plant Care _____

_____

_____

_____

Pet Care _____

_____

_____

_____

Instructions for House-Sitters

Papers _____

_____

Mail _____

_____

Garbage Day _____

_____

Recycling Day _____

_____

Oddities _____

_____

Extra Car Keys _____

Extra House Key _____

For House Problems Contact: _____

_____

Veterinarian _____

Insurance Agents _____

_____

Number To Reach Homeowner (in extreme emergency) _____

Maps and Location of the House

*Draw a map and write verbal instructions of how to get to your house.
Use these instructions for your own ready reference, and leave them with the baby-sitter
or with the house-sitter, in case emergency assistance is needed (police, fire, and rescue
teams need clear, concise directions to your home). In less urgent circumstances, copy
and send them along with invitations for social events.*

Illustration / Map

Maps and Location of the House

Written Description

Describe how to get to your house in simple, but easily understood terms.

From: _____

_____

_____

_____

_____

_____

_____

_____

_____

_____

_____

_____

_____

_____

_____

_____

_____

Maps and Location of the House

Alternative Directions

In case the usual route is unavailable, or if help comes from another direction, be prepared.

From: _____

_____

_____

_____

_____

_____

_____

_____

Illustration / Map

From:

In Case of Emergency

This is one of the most important sections of The House Diary.
Mark these pages for all family members, baby-sitters, and house guests.

Telephone Numbers

Police _____   Fire _____

Medical _____   Poison Center _____

Security _____   Neighbor _____

Ambulance _____   Hospital _____

Physician _____   Suicide Hotline _____

Neighborhood Watch _____

_____

_____

_____

This Address Is:

_____

Telephone:

_____

Directions To This Address:

See previous pages

In Case of Emergency

Location of Emergency Housing

_____

_____

_____

_____

_____

_____

_____

_____

Local Radio Emergency Broadcasts

_____

_____

_____

_____

_____

_____

_____

In Case of Emergency

Access Route if:

Flood _____

_____

Volcanic Eruption _____

_____

Mud Slide _____

_____

Forest Fire _____

_____

Ice Storm _____

_____

Earthquake _____

_____

Tornado _____

_____

Tsunami _____

_____

In Case of Fire

A plan for evacuation or for personal safety in event of a natural disaster will help prevent panic in your household and possibly save lives.

Exit Route Diagrams

Diagram an exit route from every room in the house and designate a meeting place outside. Make sure every family member understands the evacuation procedures; practice them periodically.

In Case of Fire

Exit Route Diagrams

Fire Prevention

Be prepared and stay prepared. Check your equipment frequently to be sure it's in working order and easily accessible.

Fire/Smoke Detectors

Last Inspection ▶ / Location ▼														

Fire Extinguishers

Last Inspection ▶ / Location ▼														

Fire Prevention

Fire/Smoke Detectors

Last Inspection ▶ Location ▼												

Fire Extinguishers

Last Inspection ▶ Location ▼												

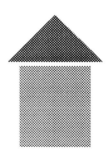

"The good neighbor looks beyond the external and discerns those inner qualities that make all men human and, therefore, brothers."
– Martin Luther King, Jr. (1929-1968)

Financial Overview

3 🏠 3

Purchase Facts

Realtor _____

Date of Purchase _____

Previous Owner(s), if known _____

_____

_____

Purchase Costs _____

_____

_____

_____

_____

_____

Important Purchase Dates _____

_____

_____

Purchase Facts

Purchase(s) made from Seller(s)

_____

_____

_____

_____

_____

_____

_____

_____

_____

_____

_____

_____

_____

_____

_____

_____

_____

_____

Yearly Fixed Costs

These grids allow you to keep a yearly account of operating costs for your house. Enter expenses each month, then at the end of the year total the rows and columns.

	January	February	March	April	May	June
Mortgage(s)						
Taxes						
Insurance						
Association Fees						
Electricity						
Garbage						
Sewer						
Gas						
Water						
Other Expenses *(such as security system, cable, yardwork)*						
Monthly Totals						

Expenses for the Year_____

July	August	September	October	November	December	TOTAL

Yearly Fixed Costs

	January	February	March	April	May	June
Mortgage(s)						
Taxes						
Insurance						
Association Fees						
Electricity						
Garbage						
Sewer						
Gas						
Water						
Other Expenses *(such as security system, cable, yardwork)*						
Monthly Totals						

Expenses for the Year_____

July	August	September	October	November	December	TOTAL

Yearly Fixed Costs

	January	February	March	April	May	June
Mortgage(s)						
Taxes						
Insurance						
Association Fees						
Electricity						
Garbage						
Sewer						
Gas						
Water						
Other Expenses *(such as security system, cable, yardwork)*						
Monthly Totals						

Expenses for the Year_____

July	August	September	October	November	December	TOTAL

Yearly Fixed Costs

	January	February	March	April	May	June
Mortgage(s)						
Taxes						
Insurance						
Association Fees						
Electricity						
Garbage						
Sewer						
Gas						
Water						
Other Expenses *(such as security system, cable, yardwork)*						
Monthly Totals						

Expenses for the Year_____

July	August	September	October	November	December	TOTAL

Yearly Fixed Costs

	January	February	March	April	May	June
Mortgage(s)						
Taxes						
Insurance						
Association Fees						
Electricity						
Garbage						
Sewer						
Gas						
Water						
Other Expenses *(such as security system, cable, yardwork)*						
Monthly Totals						

Expenses for the Year_____

July	August	September	October	November	December	TOTAL

Fixed Costs and Improvements – Yearly Total

Use these grids to calculate the total cost of running, maintaining, and improving your home.

Year _____	Amounts from Fixed Costs *previous pages*	Amounts from "The House Diary" Tax Deductible	Non-Tax Deductible	Total Fixed Costs and Improvements
January				
February				
March				
April				
May				
June				
July				
August				
September				
October				
November				
December				
Totals				

Fixed Costs and Improvements – Yearly Total

Year _____	Amounts from Fixed Costs *previous pages*	Amounts from "The House Diary"		Total Fixed Costs and Improvements
		Tax Deductible	*Non-Tax Deductible*	
January				
February				
March				
April				
May				
June				
July				
August				
September				
October				
November				
December				
Totals				

Fixed Costs and Improvements – Yearly Total

Year _____	Amounts from Fixed Costs *previous pages*	Amounts from "The House Diary"		Total Fixed Costs and Improvements
		Tax Deductible	*Non-Tax Deductible*	
January				
February				
March				
April				
May				
June				
July				
August				
September				
October				
November				
December				
Totals				

Fixed Costs and Improvements – Yearly Total

Year _____	Amounts from Fixed Costs *previous pages*	Amounts from "The House Diary"		Total Fixed Costs and Improvements
		Tax Deductible	*Non-Tax Deductible*	
January				
February				
March				
April				
May				
June				
July				
August				
September				
October				
November				
December				
Totals				

Fixed Costs and Improvements – Yearly Total

Year _____	Amounts from Fixed Costs *previous pages*	Amounts from "The House Diary"		Total Fixed Costs and Improvements
		Tax Deductible	*Non-Tax Deductible*	
January				
February				
March				
April				
May				
June				
July				
August				
September				
October				
November				
December				
Totals				

Lifetime Summary

Year	Amount

Year	Amount

Year	Amount

"A house is much more to my taste than a tree,
And for groves, oh! a good grove of chimneys for me."
– Charles Morris (1745-1838)

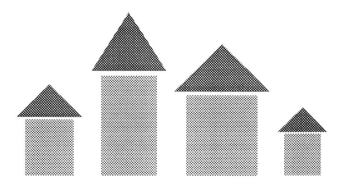

The House Resumé

The House Resumé

The House Resumé is provided so that you may update your records to the point when you begin using
The House Diary. *Old receipts, work orders, and checks will supplement your memory.*

Item	Date	Description	Cost

The House Resumé

Item	Date	Description	Cost

The House Resumé

Item	Date	Description	Cost

The House Resumé

Item	Date	Description	Cost

The House Resumé

Item	Date	Description	Cost

The House Resumé

Item	Date	Description	Cost

The House Resumé

Item	Date	Description	Cost

The House Resumé

Item	Date	Description	Cost

The House Resumé

Item	Date	Description	Cost

The House Resumé

Item	Date	Description	Cost

Fixtures in the House – Appliances & Systems

A record of fixtures is essential for insurance coverage and an easy reference if you replace an item or sell your house.

	Water Heater	Range	Refrigerator
Location			
Brand			
Model Number			
Installed by			
Date Installed			
Warranty Information			
Cost			
Serviceperson & Telephone Number			
Comments			

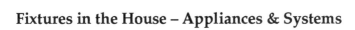

Fixtures in the House – Appliances & Systems

Security System	Washer	Dryer	Air Conditioning

Fixtures in the House – Appliances & Systems

	Garage Door Opener	Freezer	Microwave Oven
Location			
Brand			
Model Number			
Installed by			
Date Installed			
Warranty Information			
Cost			
Serviceperson & Telephone Number			
Comments			

Fixtures in the House – Appliances & Systems

Jacuzzi	Trash Compactor	Water Purifier	Heating System

Fixtures in the House – Appliances & Systems

Location			
Brand			
Model Number			
Installed by			
Date Installed			
Warranty Information			
Cost			
Serviceperson & Telephone Number			
Comments			

Fixtures in the House – Appliances & Systems

Fixtures in the House – Floor Coverings

Location			
Type/Brand			
Contents			
Installed by			
Costs			
Date Installed			
Warranty Information			
Special Care			
Comments			

Fixtures in the House – Floor Coverings

Location			
Type/Brand			
Contents			
Installed by			
Costs			
Date Installed			
Warranty Information			
Special Care			
Comments			

Fixtures in the House – Floor Coverings

Location			
Type/Brand			
Contents			
Installed by			
Costs			
Date Installed			
Warranty Information			
Special Care			
Comments			

Fixtures in the House – Floor Coverings

Location			
Type/Brand			
Contents			
Installed by			
Costs			
Date Installed			
Warranty Information			
Special Care			
Comments			

Fixtures in the House – Wall Coverings

Location			
Type/Brand			
Contents			
Installed by			
Costs			
Date Installed			
Warranty Information			
Special Care			
Comments			

Fixtures in the House – Wall Coverings

Location			
Type/Brand			
Contents			
Installed by			
Costs			
Date Installed			
Warranty Information			
Special Care			
Comments			

Fixtures in the House – Wall Coverings

Location			
Type/Brand			
Contents			
Installed by			
Costs			
Date Installed			
Warranty Information			
Special Care			
Comments			

Fixtures in the House – Wall Coverings

Location			
Type/Brand			
Contents			
Installed by			
Costs			
Date Installed			
Warranty Information			
Special Care			
Comments			

Fixtures in the House – Window Coverings

Location			
Type/Brand			
Contents			
Installed by			
Costs			
Date Installed			
Warranty Information			
Special Care			
Comments			

Fixtures in the House – Window Coverings

Location			
Type/Brand			
Contents			
Installed by			
Costs			
Date Installed			
Warranty Information			
Special Care			
Comments			

Fixtures in the House – Window Coverings

Location			
Type/Brand			
Contents			
Installed by			
Costs			
Date Installed			
Warranty Information			
Special Care			
Comments			

Fixtures in the House – Window Coverings

Location			
Type/Brand			
Contents			
Installed by			
Costs			
Date Installed			
Warranty Information			
Special Care			
Comments			

"La maison est une machine à habiter." (*A house is a living machine.*)

— Le Corbusier (1887-1965)

The House Diary

5 5

The House Diary

Here is the heart of The House Diary – *a running record of the day-to-day, week-to-week, or incident-to-incident workings of your house. It has been designed to be as flexible as possible, in order to meet each homeowner's individual needs.*

Helpful hint: keep guarantees and warranties, paint samples, pieces of wallpaper, and so on in one place, such as a box or a drawer. Having them all in one location makes them easier to find and harder to lose. It will save you from having to hunt for them before you start that next project.

Below are examples of the entries I have kept since learning my house needed that new roof.

Item	Date	Description	Cost	I
Garage door	11-10-91	Replaced old door for 3 section aluminum door		
		Alpine Door	$95.00	✔
Chimney cleaned	12-15-91	Black Hat Co. 555-7777	$45.00	
Oven	12-17-91	Replaced lower element in oven		
		Pac. El. (Don) 555-1111	$79.00	

The House Diary

Make entries in The House Diary *just as you would in a personal journal. The column labeled "Item" will provide easy reference when you need to track past improvements and repairs done on the house. Other information to record for each job could include: what was done; who did the work and the telephone number; names of suppliers; quantity of material used, and quality of the work; colors, cost, and other remarks on the job. In the column labeled "I" indicate whether the job is a tax deductible expense.*

Item	Date	Description	Cost	I

The House Diary

Item	Date	Description	Cost	I

The House Diary

Item	Date	Description	Cost	I

The House Diary

Item	Date	Description	Cost	I

The House Diary

Item	Date	Description	Cost	I

The House Diary

Item	Date	Description	Cost	I

The House Diary

Item	Date	Description	Cost	I

The House Diary

Item	Date	Description	Cost	I

The House Diary

Item	Date	Description	Cost	I

The House Diary

Item	Date	Description	Cost	I

The House Diary

Item	Date	Description	Cost	I

The House Diary

Item	Date	Description	Cost	I

The House Diary

Item	Date	Description	Cost	I

The House Diary

Item	Date	Description	Cost	I

The House Diary

Item	Date	Description	Cost	I

The House Diary

Item	Date	Description	Cost	I

The House Diary

Item	Date	Description	Cost	I

The House Diary

Item	Date	Description	Cost	I

The House Diary

Item	Date	Description	Cost	I

The House Diary

Item	Date	Description	Cost	I

The House Diary

Item	Date	Description	Cost	I

The House Diary

Item	Date	Description	Cost	I

The House Diary

Item	Date	Description	Cost	I

The House Diary

Item	Date	Description	Cost	I

THE HOUSE DIARY

The House Diary

Item	Date	Description	Cost	I

The House Diary

Item	Date	Description	Cost	I

The House Diary

Item	Date	Description	Cost	I

The House Diary

Item	Date	Description	Cost	I

The House Diary

Item	Date	Description	Cost	I

The House Diary

Item	Date	Description	Cost	I

The House Diary

Item	Date	Description	Cost	I

The House Diary

Item	Date	Description	Cost	I

The House Diary

Item	Date	Description	Cost	I

The House Diary

Item	Date	Description	Cost	I

The House Diary

Item	Date	Description	Cost	I

The House Diary

Item	Date	Description	Cost	I

The House Diary

Item	Date	Description	Cost	I

The House Diary

Item	Date	Description	Cost	I

The House Diary

Item	Date	Description	Cost	I

The House Diary

Item	Date	Description	Cost	I

The House Diary

Item	Date	Description	Cost	I

The House Diary

Item	Date	Description	Cost	I

The House Diary

Item	Date	Description	Cost	I

The House Diary

Item	Date	Description	Cost	I

The House Diary

Item	Date	Description	Cost	I

The House Diary

Item	Date	Description	Cost	I

The House Diary

Item	Date	Description	Cost	I

The House Diary

Item	Date	Description	Cost	I

THE HOUSE DIARY

The House Diary

Item	Date	Description	Cost	I

The House Diary

Item	Date	Description	Cost	I

The House Diary

Item	Date	Description	Cost	I

The House Diary

Item	Date	Description	Cost	I

The House Diary

Item	Date	Description	Cost	I

The House Diary

Item	Date	Description	Cost	I

THE HOUSE DIARY

The House Diary

Item	Date	Description	Cost	I

The House Diary

Item	Date	Description	Cost	I

The House Diary

Item	Date	Description	Cost	I

The House Diary

Item	Date	Description	Cost	I

THE HOUSE DIARY

The House Diary

Item	Date	Description	Cost	I

The House Diary

Item	Date	Description	Cost	I

The House Diary

Item	Date	Description	Cost	I

The House Diary

Item	Date	Description	Cost	I

The House Diary

Item	Date	Description	Cost	I

The House Diary

Item	Date	Description	Cost	I

The House Diary

Item	Date	Description	Cost	I

The House Diary

Item	Date	Description	Cost	I

The House Diary

Item	Date	Description	Cost	I

The House Diary

Item	Date	Description	Cost	I

The House Diary

Item	Date	Description	Cost	I

The House Diary

Item	Date	Description	Cost	I

The House Diary

Item	Date	Description	Cost	I

The House Diary

Item	Date	Description	Cost	I

The House Diary

Item	Date	Description	Cost	I

The House Diary

Item	Date	Description	Cost	I

The House Diary

Item	Date	Description	Cost	I

"I hope you are using and benefiting from your copy of **THE HOUSE DIARY**. *Here is an easy way for you to help friends simplify their house record-keeping, and* **THE HOUSE DIARY** *makes a great moving, house-warming, or wedding gift. Please let me hear from you. I would be delighted to know how you are using* **THE HOUSE DIARY**."*

Lottie K. Brelsford

ORDER FORM

Mail orders to: Wow • Wadda, Co.
P.O. Box 12223
Portland, OR 97212

THE HOUSE DIARY. $16.95*

Please send _____ copies.

Total Order $_____

Shipping and Handling _____

(Add $2.00 for the first book and
$.75 for each additional book. U.S. orders)

TOTAL PAYMENT $_____

Two convenient ways to pay:

❑ Check or money order enclosed

❑ Please charge my credit card: ❑ Mastercard   ❑ Visa   Exp date _____

Credit card number: ☐☐☐☐☐☐☐☐☐☐☐☐☐☐☐☐

Signature _____

Telephone number (include area code) _____

Name _____

Address _____

City/State _____ Zip Code _____

*For orders of 10 or more copies, please telephone for discount information (503) 249-0051.